# Golden Rule

Have you ever stop and ask yourself where do I want to be in one year, three years or even five years? If so are you clear about your objectives at the moment? Do you even know what you want to achieve by the end of the week let along the end of the month?

If you want to succeed at ANYTHING you must set goals. Without goals you lack focus and direction, you're merely flowing through life. Goal setting is essential to be the success that lives in all of us. To accomplish goals, however, you need to learn how to set them. You can't simply say, "I want to sell real estate" and never set any goals on how and where to start the process.

# What are goals

A goal is an idea or desired result that a person or a group of people envisions, plans and commits to achieve. People endeavor to reach goals within a finite time by setting deadlines.

# Goal Setting

Setting clear, obtainable goals are vital to the success of your brand/business. To maximize your full potential and get outstanding results you will need to set goals that are reachable, clear and precise on what vision your brand is trying to represent. For example, if you want to buy a building it needs to be a set amount you are willing to spend on it, you need to have a specific square foot amount for space.

First, we must evaluate your current analysis to understand where your brand is at this very moment. Even if your brand is just a thought, it means you are in the process of building and at least color schemes and techniques should be in place. Here are a few questions to ask yourself right now……..

What is my target audience?
Whom am I trying to reach?
What product/service am I trying to sell?
What can I currently be doing to bring awareness to my brand?

These are just a few quick questions to ask yourself about the brand that you are representing.

# What are your goals?

Make sure you separate your long-term and short-term goals. Short term goals are any goals that are clear and obtainable within six months any other goal will be a long-term goal.

Ex. Short-term goals are to write another book within six months, long-term goal will be turning that book into a movie or short tv series

- If you're a writer, your goal is to write a book
- If you're a runner, your goal may be to run a marathon
- If you're an entrepreneur, your goal is to build a million-dollar business

Could have made an excuse, INSTEAD, I made a way

# What will my brand achieve in

## 3 months

## 6 months

## 9 months

## 12 months

# Setting Goals in Writing

I have a motto to achieve your goals you must keep them in front of you. I have three planners (I know that's obsessive) but all three have the different things I need to accomplish for the week, month, and year. I also carry a little pocket pouch in my purse it has in it my long-term goals as well as my goals for the whole year. I have my goals written on index cards almost like affirmations and I read them daily- three times a day.

# Setting Goals in Writing

The physical act of writing your goals down makes them real and there are no excuses to be made once they are written. When writing them down make sure you use the word "will" instead of "will like to do", "see can I", "going to". For example, I will write three books by December 30, 2019, by 11 am EST. My goals have a date, the amount as well as an exact time. My goal is reachable and tangible. I can now write this affirmation down on a goal card and place it in my purse.

# Goals

What exactly are your goals? To set them you need to be specific all the way down to the measurement of a home or the color of a vehicle. Name some goals that you have for the next few months?

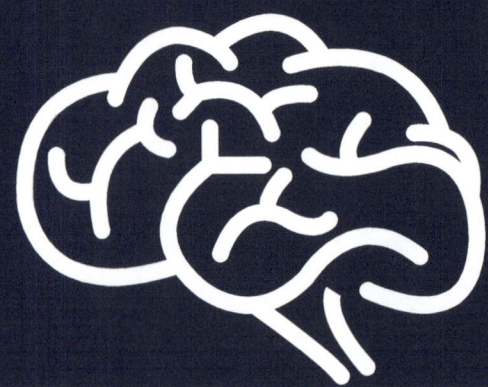

# Goal Worksheet

My goal is:

Goal completion date:

Steps to reaching my goals:

Tools to help me reach my goals:

# Goal Worksheet

My goal is:

Goal completion date:

Steps to reaching my goals:

Tools to help me reach my goals:

# Goal Worksheet

My goal is:

Goal completion date:

Steps to reaching my goals:

Tools to help me reach my goals:

*To succeed you must have stickability!*

# Mesmerizing Goal Planning

## Monthly Goals

## Weekly Goals

## Daily Goals

# Goals, Plans and Execution

Goals are great, but in order to achieve them there has to be a plan in motion. To execute your goals, they must be broken down into smaller goals that are obtainable. Once you have broken your goal down into a smaller goal than you must create an execution plan. For example: I will write three books in 2019 (goal) by December 31, 2019, at 11 am EST. In order to achieve this goal, I will write one book every 120 days (smaller goal) by creating a twenty-day challenge that I must write two thousand words a day for twenty days (execution).

# Strategic Planning

Even with a goal, plan, and execution in place, your goals must be realistic. If I set a goal to make $100,000 in a month and never earned that amount in a year, that goal can seem unrealistic, even with a clear plan and execution it will be hard to obtain. Begin with small steps towards your goal with plans to increase your income by $2,000 a month and so forth. During this time you will create a plan that will eventually lead you to make the $100,000 a year or monthly whatever the goal may be.

*Making it impossible for your target audience to choose anyone else- period.*

# Branding While Planning

The purpose of marketing your brand is to get your target audience to choose you over anyone else. Knowing what your audience need places your products first on their list. Launch your brand and not the product, get others use to your brand and the things you offer such as the products will follow.

# What exactly is branding?

Branding is one of the most important parts of any business, whether big or small. Your brand is simply a promise to your customers on the products/services you offer. It's defining who you are and how you want to be perceived. It tells your customer what to expect from your products/service and how you're different from your competitors.

# Branding 101

## *Know yourself*

What am I here for? No really, why does the world need your product. Why did you create it? How is your service any different from your competitors? How do you want people to feel when they interact with your brand? What is it you want your customers to take away from interacting with your brand?

# Branding 101

< Know your audience>
-Define your target audience- age group, demographics, lifestyle etc.
-Who needs your product/service?
-Find your niche and focus solely on that. You can't be everything to everyone know you.
-Do your data research understand your audience as well as products/services.

# The Message, Mission, and Meaningful

Your brand should be clear to everyone who encounters your product/service. Creating a mission statement helps to bring awareness to your brand. The mission statement should be one you believe in and live by. Also, create a tagline that's both meaningful and memorable.

# Brand Communication

This is the foundation of your brand, communication to the masses. Your logo, website, business card, gift cards, packaging, promotional materials are ways you communicate your brand to the world. You should have a brand color scheme also which is how others can identify your brand, whatever you choose stick to them; use these colors when creating content, logos, website material etc.

# Brand Focus

Focus on your brand and what you offer.

> Clear brand details and the products/service that you offer
> Write down your brand message
> Create a voice for your company that can be seen visually

"Don't compare your brand to others. There's no comparison between the sun and the moon, they shine when it's their time"

# Brand Strategy

Since we know our target audience and know what they want such as products/services now is the time to deliver your message, you guess right, advertising. Your brand strategy is how, what, where and when you plan on communicating to your target audience what you have to offer them that is beneficial.

# Brand Strategy

Stay Alert to what is happening around you. There are certain situations that will create different opportunities. How prepared are you? Once an opportunity is recognized act upon it, seize the moment to create which is what you are known to do. There are very few people that see an opportunity and act upon because of fear or they believe they can't achieve it. How do you seize opportunities?

# I am my Brand!

It's not whom you know, it's who knows you. Build your personal brand and customers will be loyal to you. In sales, a customer buys from a salesperson first before the brand. You are "The" brand and your dedication and self- belief will help with the product that you are selling

# Personal Branding

*Create your product
*Build a business community
*Be an expert
*Set yourself apart from the competition
* Develop a professional image
*Market yourself
*Become a resource
*Collaborate with other brands
*Be the best at what you do

# Brand Plan

A successful brand plan must identify consumer targets and the demographic in which the business needs to support its brand. There must be a clear message to entice these consumers to buy the product. Those messages are what your brand and products can do that no other company nor its products can do things.

# Start By STARTING! Yes You!

# How to start anything

Decision – The first thing is to decide on what you want. Making a decision is something you must look deep into yourself on what it is that you want. The decision-making process is not easy, especially when making life-changing ones. What is it that you have been postponing that you really want to do? Once you decide on what you want later, classify it as a goal to achieve. Eliminate choices by setting standards that are attainable to the decision being made.

# Goal Setting

Consistency- If there is one word I will use all year consistency will be it. You must be consistent with the decision that has been made. Getting rid of distractions such as people, phones when working as well as social media accounts are great ways to start anything.

# Goal Setting

Roadblocks- There will always be stabling blocks in the way but with a solid plan for the decision that was made, one will be able to overcome just about anything. Roadblocks let's just cross them, stumble past them and get back to work.

# Setting Goals in Writing

Follow through– Following through is being consistent in a nutshell. Not only do you have to be consistent you must stay in your element on the decision that you have made. Follow through with what you stated you wanted, find the resources, create a goal chart and get to work.

# Discipline

Real Discipline- To have real discipline one must train. With training, it's preparing for whatever it is that you want. You must research and find resources to complete the task at hand. Take action because nothing happens until you make a move.

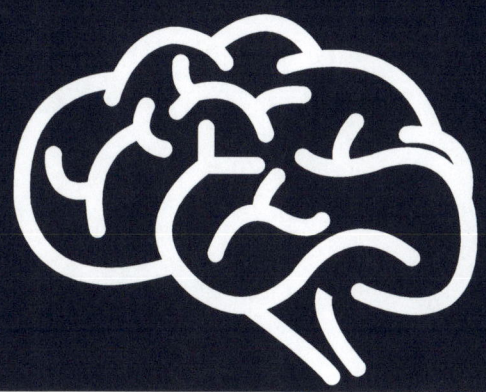

# Discipline

To start something just simply make the decision of what it is that you want. Also get a clear understanding of what it will take to achieve that goal, stay consistent and get to work. Remember nothing moves until you choose. Make a plan and stick to it- no matter what.

# Proper Planning

Success can occur at any given moment and time of day. Since we don't know what day it will occur, it's best to plan that day will be every day. Proper planning for the day is essential for success, especially with no two days being the same. Plan with the goals that you have set for yourself. Have you set your goals? Are they in front of you every day?

# Environment

The right space can create magic. The space in which you work creates the success you will have. Create the environment you want will encourage you to keep going even on one of your worse days. This includes surrounding yourself around people who get it. Your support system will make the road for success less bumpy. It's up to you to create a great work environment.

# Risk Factor

We all know the saying "No risk, No Reward", but I like to say no risk there will be no nothing. Taking chances are vital to anything that one does. Imagine when you were a baby trying to walk, the risk of falling was there, but you got up and did it anyway, numerous times until you were able to walk. The same method applies in business. Take risks and do them often, don't let the fear of the unknown stop you from believing.

"A dream is just a dream until it is written down, and it becomes a goal"
-Emmitt Smith

# THE CEO GOAL PLANNER

PRAY..PLAN...PROSPER

CONSISTENCY IS SETTING A STANDARD, CREATING A HABIT FOR YOURSELF, FIGHTING DISTRACTIONS, ALIGNING PATTERNS, STICKING WITH YOUR GOALS. REMEMBER, THEY'RE YOUR DREAMS!

NO ONE OWES YOU ANYTHING!

# THE CEO GOAL PLANNER

**TOP THREE GOALS**

**TO-DO LIST**

**NOTES**

**OPPORTUNITIES**

**QUOTE OF THE DAY**

**REMINDERS**

# THE CEO GOAL PLANNER

**TOP THREE GOALS**

**TO-DO LIST**

**NOTES**

**OPPORTUNITIES**

**QUOTE OF THE DAY**

**REMINDERS**

# THE CEO GOAL PLANNER

**TOP THREE GOALS**

**TO-DO LIST**

**NOTES**

**OPPORTUNITIES**

**QUOTE OF THE DAY**

**REMINDERS**

# The Ceo Goal Planner Notes

- [ ] _____
- [ ] _____
- [ ] _____
- [ ] _____
- [ ] _____
- [ ] _____

# The Ceo Planner Notes

# The CEO Planner Notes

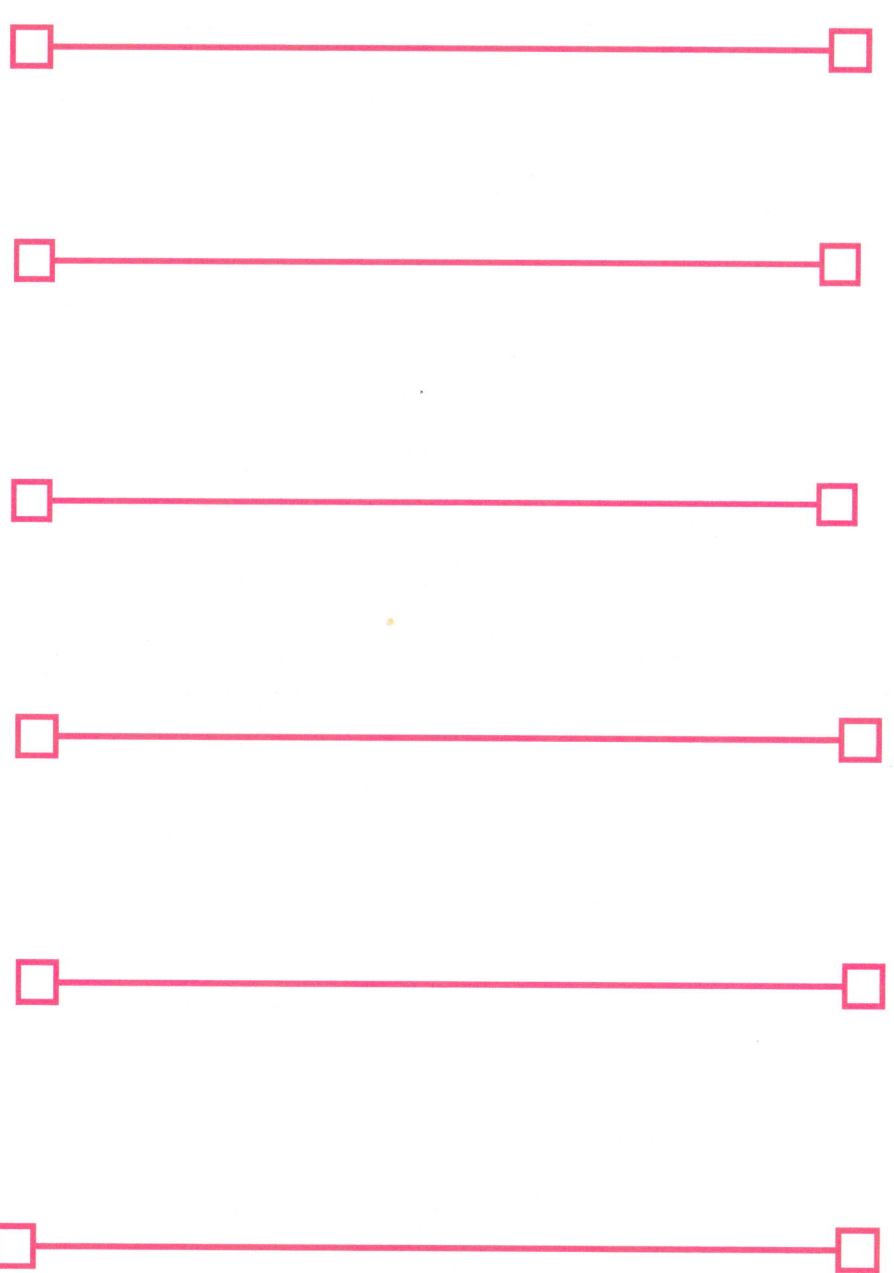

MONTHLY PLANNER

## MONTHLY FOCUS

☐ ..................................
☐ ..................................
☐ ..................................
☐ ..................................
☐ ..................................

## DATES TO REMEMBER

..................................
..................................
..................................
..................................
..................................

## NOTES

## GOALS

☐ ..................................
☐ ..................................
☐ ..................................
☐ ..................................
☐ ..................................
☐ ..................................
☐ ..................................
☐ ..................................
☐ ..................................
☐ ..................................
☐ ..................................

# MONTHLY PLANNER

## MONTHLY FOCUS

- ☐ ....................................
- ☐ ....................................
- ☐ ....................................
- ☐ ....................................
- ☐ ....................................

## DATES TO REMEMBER

....................................
....................................
....................................
....................................
....................................

## NOTES

## GOALS

- ☐ ....................................
- ☐ ....................................
- ☐ ....................................
- ☐ ....................................
- ☐ ....................................
- ☐ ....................................
- ☐ ....................................
- ☐ ....................................
- ☐ ....................................
- ☐ ....................................
- ☐ ....................................

MONTHLY PLANNER

## MONTHLY FOCUS

- ☐ ..................................
- ☐ ..................................
- ☐ ..................................
- ☐ ..................................
- ☐ ..................................

## DATES TO REMEMBER

..................................
..................................
..................................
..................................
..................................

## NOTES

## GOALS

- ☐ ..................................
- ☐ ..................................
- ☐ ..................................
- ☐ ..................................
- ☐ ..................................
- ☐ ..................................
- ☐ ..................................
- ☐ ..................................
- ☐ ..................................
- ☐ ..................................
- ☐ ..................................

MONTHLY PLANNER

## MONTHLY FOCUS

- ☐ ....................................
- ☐ ....................................
- ☐ ....................................
- ☐ ....................................
- ☐ ....................................

## DATES TO REMEMBER

....................................
....................................
....................................
....................................
....................................

## NOTES

## GOALS

- ☐ ....................................
- ☐ ....................................
- ☐ ....................................
- ☐ ....................................
- ☐ ....................................
- ☐ ....................................
- ☐ ....................................
- ☐ ....................................
- ☐ ....................................
- ☐ ....................................
- ☐ ....................................

MONTHLY PLANNER

MONTHLY FOCUS

- ☐ ..................................
- ☐ ..................................
- ☐ ..................................
- ☐ ..................................
- ☐ ..................................

Dates to Remember

..................................
..................................
..................................
..................................
..................................

NOTES

GOALS

- ☐ ..................................
- ☐ ..................................
- ☐ ..................................
- ☐ ..................................
- ☐ ..................................
- ☐ ..................................
- ☐ ..................................
- ☐ ..................................
- ☐ ..................................
- ☐ ..................................
- ☐ ..................................

 # Brainstorming

 # Brainstorming

Don't focus on anyone's success but your own. It doesn't matter how appealing their lives might seem. There is no success without sacrifice. Are you ready?

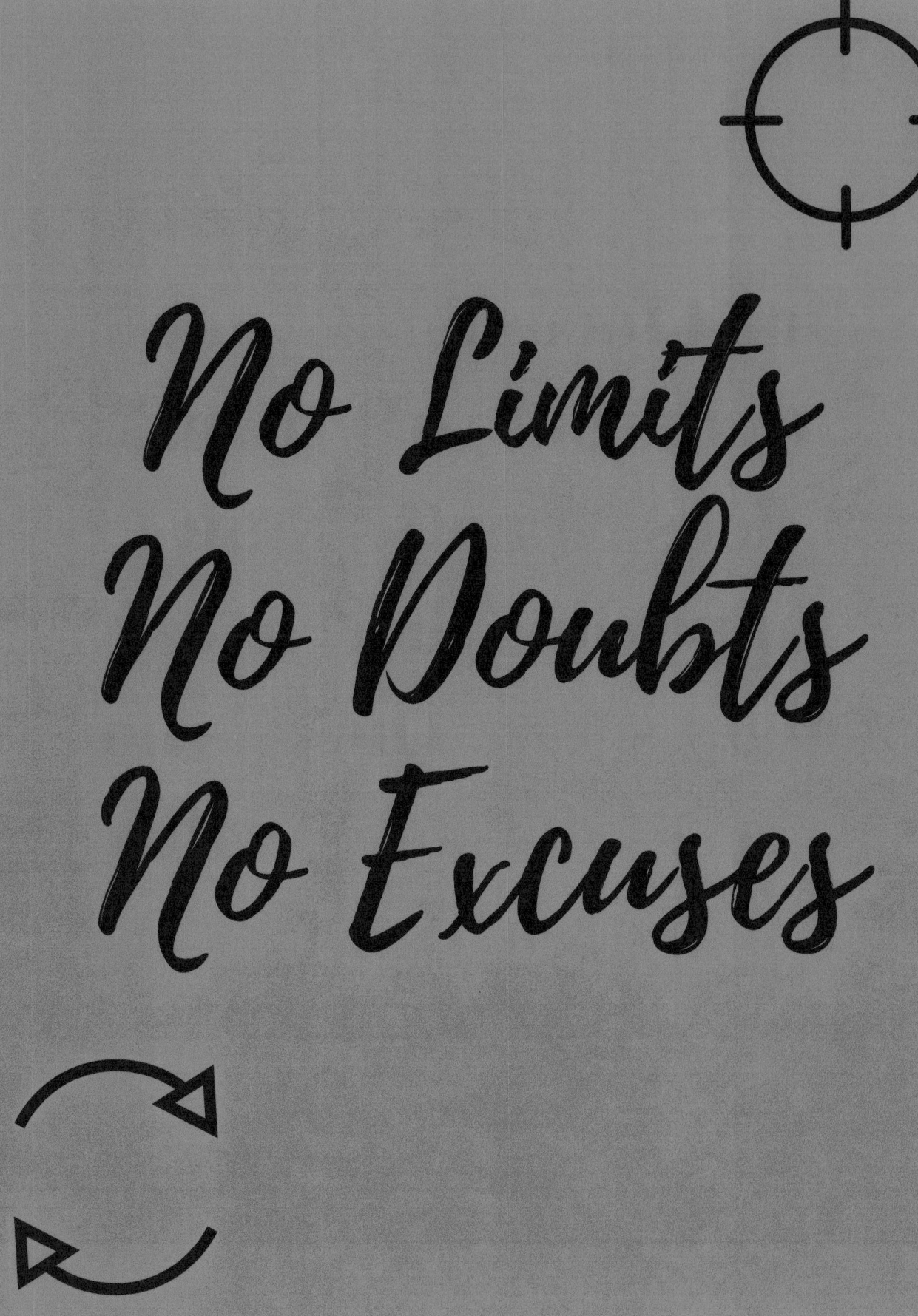

Create by:

*Malkia Miko*

Out Dream Yourself

www.ingramcontent.com/pod-product-compliance
Lightning Source LLC
Chambersburg PA
CBHW042322250526
R18347200002B/R183472PG45473CBX00012B/15